MONTROSE-CRESCENTA

D0787689

APACHE
History and Culture

Helen Dwyer and D. L. Birchfield

Consultant Robert J. Conley
Sequoyah Distinguished Professor at Western Carolina University

Gareth Stevens
Publishing

Please visit our website, **www.garethstevens.com**. For a free color catalog of all our high-quality books, call toll free 1-800-542-2595 or fax 1-877-542-2596.

Library of Congress Cataloging-in-Publication Data

Birchfield, D. L., 1948-
Apache history and culture / D. L. Birchfield and Helen Dwyer.
    p. cm. — (Native American library)
Includes index.
ISBN 978-1-4339-6662-0 (pbk.)
ISBN 978-1-4339-6663-7 (6-pack)
ISBN 978-1-4339-6661-3 (library binding)
1. Apache Indians—History. 2. Apache Indians—Social life and customs. I. Dwyer, Helen. II. Title.
E99.A6B57 2012
979.004'9725—dc22
                                    2011016310

New edition published in 2012 by
Gareth Stevens Publishing
111 East 14th Street, Suite 349
New York, NY 10003

First edition published 2005 by Gareth Stevens Publishing

Copyright © 2012 Gareth Stevens Publishing

Produced by Discovery Books
Project editor: Helen Dwyer
Designer and page production: Sabine Beaupré
Photo researchers: Tom Humphrey and Helen Dwyer
Maps: Stefan Chabluk

Photo credits: Corbis: pp. 11, 13 (top), 18, 22, 24 (bottom), 31, 32, 39; Gary Zahm/U.S. Fish and Wildlife Service: 29; Native Stock: pp. 13 (bottom), 23 (both), 24 (top), 26, 27, 30, 33, 34, 36, 37; North Wind Picture Archives: pp. 12, 14; Peter Newark's American Pictures: pp. 10, 15, 16, 17, 19, 20, 21, 25; Shutterstock: pp. 5 (Caitlin Mirra), 28 (Cathy Keifer); Wikimedia: pp.7, 8 (Frank A. Rinehart).

Printed in the United States of America

CPSIA compliance information: Batch #CW12GS: For further information contact Gareth Stevens, New York, New York at 1-800-542-2595.

CONTENTS

Words that appear in the glossary are printed in **boldface** type the first time they appear in the text.

INTRODUCTION

The Apaches are a people of the southwestern United States and northern Mexico. They are just one of the many groups of Native Americans who live today in North America. There are well over five hundred Native American tribes in the United States and more than six hundred in Canada. At least three million people in North America consider themselves to be Native Americans. But who are Native Americans, and how do the Apaches fit into the history of North America's native peoples?

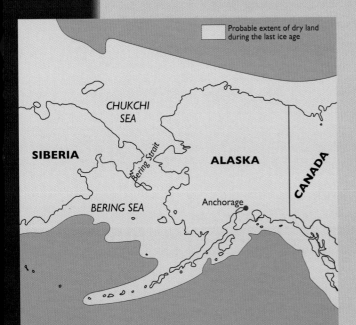

Siberia (Asia) and Alaska (North America) are today separated by an area of ocean named the Bering Strait. During the last ice age, the green area on this map was at times dry land. The Asian ancestors of the Apaches walked from one continent to the other.

THE FIRST IMMIGRANTS

Native Americans are people whose **ancestors** settled in North America thousands of years ago. These ancestors probably came from eastern parts of Asia. Their **migrations** probably occurred during cold periods called **ice ages**. At these times, sea levels were much lower than they are now. The area between northeastern Asia and Alaska was dry land, so it was possible to walk between the continents.

Scientists are not sure when these migrations took place, but it must have been more than twelve thousand years ago. Around that time, water levels rose and covered the land between Asia and the Americas. The peoples who spoke

Athabascan languages, such as the Apaches, are believed to have been among the most recent of these arrivals in North America.

By around ten thousand years ago, the climate had warmed and was similar to conditions today. The first peoples in North America moved around the continent in small groups, hunting wild animals and collecting a wide variety of plant foods. Gradually these groups spread out and lost contact with each other. They developed separate **cultures** and adopted lifestyles that suited their **environments.**

The Cliff Palace at Mesa Verde, Colorado, is the most spectacular example of Native American culture that survives today. It consists of more than 150 rooms and pits built around A.D. 1200 from sandstone blocks.

SETTLING DOWN

Although many tribes continued to gather food and hunt or fish, some Native Americans began to live in settlements and grow crops. Their homes ranged from underground pit houses and huts of mud and thatch to dwellings in cliffs. By 3500 B.C., a plentiful supply of fish in the Pacific Ocean and in rivers had enabled people to settle in large coastal villages from Alaska to Washington State. In the deserts of Arizona more than two thousand years later, farmers constructed hundreds of miles of **irrigation** canals to carry water to their crops. The Apaches may have arrived in this region as early as A.D. 800 or as late as the fifteenth century. By the 1500s, the Eastern Apaches were hunting on the southern Great Plains and trading with the Pueblo Indians. The Western Apaches survived in small groups in a desert landscape, harvesting wild foods.

In the Ohio River valley between 700 B.C. and A.D. 500, people of the Adena and Hopewell cultures built clusters of large burial mounds, such as the Serpent Mound in Ohio, which survives today. In the Mississippi **floodplains**, the native peoples formed complex societies. They created mud and thatch temples on top of flat earth pyramids. Their largest town, Cahokia, in Illinois, contained more than one hundred mounds and may have been home to thirty thousand people.

CONTACT WITH EUROPEANS

Around A.D. 1500, European ships reached North America. The first explorers were the Spanish. Armed with guns and riding horses, they took over land and forced the Native Americans to work for them. By 1540, they had come into contact with Apache groups in the Southwest. The Spanish were followed by the British, Dutch, and French, who were looking for land to settle and for opportunities to trade.

When Native Americans met these Europeans they came into contact with diseases, such as smallpox and measles, that they had never experienced before. At least one half of all Native Americans, and possibly many more than that, were unable to overcome these diseases and died.

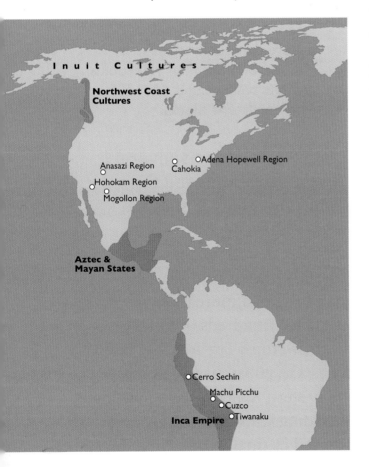

This map highlights some of the main early Native American cultures.

An Apache camp in Arizona in the late nineteenth century.

Guns were also disastrous for Native Americans. At first, only the Europeans had guns, which enabled them to overcome native peoples in fights and battles. Eventually, Native American groups obtained guns and used them in conflicts with each other. Native American groups were also forced to take sides and fight in wars between the French and British.

Horses, too, had a big influence in Native American lifestyles, especially on the Great Plains. Some groups became horse breeders and traders. People were able to travel greater distances and began to hunt buffalo on horseback. Soon horses became central to Plains trade and social life. From the early 1700s, the Comanches had begun using horses and they migrated to the southern Great Plains. They drove the Apaches west into mountainous areas of present-day New Mexico.

At the end of the 1700s, people of European descent began to migrate over the Appalachian Mountains, looking for new land to farm and exploit. By the middle of the nineteenth century, they had reached the west coast of North America. This expansion was disastrous for Native Americans. From the mid-nineteenth century, the United States claimed Apache land.

RESERVATION LIFE

Many peoples, including the Apaches, were pressured into moving onto **reservations**. The biggest of these reservations later became the U.S. state of Oklahoma. Native Americans who tried to remain in their homelands were attacked and defeated. The last of the Apaches who resisted were finally defeated in 1886.

New laws in the United States and Canada took away most of the control Native Americans had over their lives. They were expected to give up their cultures and adopt the ways and habits of white Americans. It became a crime to practice their traditional religions. Children were taken from their homes and placed in **boarding schools**, where they were forbidden to speak their native languages.

Despite this **persecution**, many Native Americans clung on to their cultures through the first half of the twentieth century. The Society of American Indians was founded in 1911 and its campaign for U.S. citizenship for Native Americans was successful in 1924. Other Native American organizations were formed to promote traditional cultures and to campaign politically for Native American rights.

Two young men on the San Carlos Apache Reservation in 1898.

The Road to Self-Government

Despite these campaigns, Native Americans on reservations endured **poverty** and very low standards of living. Many of them moved away to work and live in cities, where they hoped life would be better. In most cases, they found life just as difficult. They not only faced **discrimination** and **prejudice** but also could not compete successfully for jobs against more established ethnic groups.

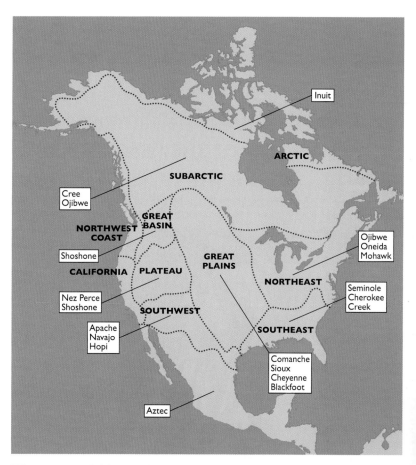

This map of North America highlights the main Native American cultural groups, along with the smaller groups, or tribes, featured in this series of books.

In the 1970s, the American Indian Movement (AIM) organized large protests that attracted attention worldwide. They highlighted the problems of unemployment, discrimination, and poverty that Native Americans experienced in North America.

The AIM protests led to changes in policy. Some new laws protected the civil rights of Native Americans, while other laws allowed tribal governments to be formed. Today tribal governments have a wide range of powers. They operate large businesses and run their own schools and health care.

Chapter 1

LAND AND ORIGINS

LAND OF THE APACHES

The Apaches are a North American native people whose historic homeland included a large portion of today's U.S. Southwest and northern Mexico. Today, tens of thousands of Apaches live in the United States, mostly in Oklahoma, New Mexico, and Arizona.

This Jicarilla Apache man was photographed in 1904 by Edward S. Curtis.

APACHE ORIGIN STORY

Little is known for certain about how the Apaches and other Native Americans got to North America. In most native cultures, stories of their people's origins have been told for generations. Apache origin stories tell of heroes coming from beneath the earth, led by Changing Woman (sometimes called White-painted Woman), who had magic powers. Helped by a spirit known as Life Giver, Changing Woman and other heroes fought monsters and made the earth safe for humans. The stories have great significance for Apache culture.

The Apaches' homelands once stretched from northern Mexico to Colorado.

In New Mexico, Apaches occupied land that had been abandoned by the ancient Mogollon people. These Mogollon ruins are at Gila Cliff Dwellings National Monument in New Mexico.

APACHES ON THE MOVE

Most scholars believe Apaches migrated from the north, arriving in the Southwest region of today's Arizona and New Mexico perhaps as early as A.D. 800 or 900. Others think the Apaches might have arrived in the Southwest after the great **drought** of the late 1300s. The drought caused ancient **civilizations** of the region, including a people called the Mogollon, to abandon most of the area and move their farming villages near big rivers, where they could rely on getting water. The Apaches would have moved in and replaced them.

THE APACHE LANGUAGE

The name Apache derives from a Zuni Pueblo Indian word meaning "enemy." The Apaches call themselves *Dene*, meaning "The People." The Apache language has six **dialects**: Chiricahua, Jicarilla, Kiowa-Apache, Lipan, Mescalero, and Western Apache.

Apache Words

Apache	Pronunciation	English
gah	gah	rabbit
beso	bay so	coin
cho	choh	large
chaa	chah	beaver
kih	key	building
tu	too	water
doo	doh	spring
nada	nah dah	corn

Chapter 2

LIFE IN THE SOUTHWEST

Before the Spanish began exploring the Southwest in the 1540s, the Eastern Apaches were the lords of the southern Great Plains, with its large herds of buffalo. Mainly a trading people, the Plains Apaches held large annual trade fairs with the Pueblo Indians of New Mexico at the eastern edge of the Great Plains. For several weeks each fall, Apaches from all across the southern Plains traded their buffalo meat and hides to the Pueblos in exchange for corn and pottery.

It has been estimated that there were once more than 70 million buffalo on the Great Plains. The buffalo, and many other animals, including elk and deer, provided for many of the Plains Apaches' needs.

THE WESTERN APACHES ADAPT

For the Western Apaches, however, west of the Rio Grande, there were no buffalo herds, only a rugged, desert wasteland that no one else wanted. Here, the Apaches proved themselves one of the most **adaptable** people in the world. They discovered and harvested the few food plants of the landscape, such as mescal. Since the land provided so little food, the Apaches had to spread thinly across the land, breaking up into small, independent units of related families.

During most of the year, the Eastern Plains Apaches hunted and traveled together in similar units. Neither the Eastern nor the Western Apaches formed any kind of national government that other nations could do business with. This situation made it impossible for the Spanish, Mexicans, and Americans who later came to the region to enter into **treaties** with the whole Apache Nation.

Mescal was made from the bulb of an agave plant, dug from the ground and stripped to its heart.

Mescal, Food of the Desert

Apaches harvested mescal in May and June. At the center of this large plant was the heart, a large white bulb 2 or 3 feet (60 to 90 centimeters) around. About 2,000 pounds (900 kilograms) of mescal would be cooked at one time in the bottom of a big pit lined with stones, on which fires were built. The food's flavor was similar to molasses, with a syrupy, sticky, fibrous texture. It could also be dried in thin strips, making a food source that would last a long time.

Dried mescal was carried in leather pouches by Apache warriors for trail food. It was lightweight and would last a long time without spoiling.

THE SPANISH AND MEXICAN ERAS

Beginning with Francisco de Coronado in the 1540s, Spanish explorers in the sixteenth century left accounts of the annual Apache trade fairs with the Pueblo Indians. When the Spanish settled New Mexico in 1598, however, they imposed taxes on the Pueblos that left them without anything to trade with the Apaches. The annual Apache trade fairs came to an end, forever changing the **economy** of the Plains Apaches.

Another huge change came when the Comanche Nation migrated south. Beginning in the early 1700s, they traveled from Wyoming to the southern Great Plains because they wanted to control the southern buffalo herds. Within a few decades, the Comanches drove the Plains Apaches from the area. About 1724, the Comanches and Apaches fought a great battle on the Plains, which the Apaches lost. Most of the Plains Apaches were driven

When the Spanish entered the Southwest, they forced the Indians to work for them. Indian life in the region would never be the same.

Francisco de Coronado, in the 1540s, was the first European to meet the Plains Apaches and the Pueblo Indians of New Mexico. He was disappointed that he didn't find the gold he was looking for.

west, into the mountains of New Mexico. Only two Apache tribes were able to stay on the buffalo plains. The Lipan Apaches stayed south of the Comanches, in far south Texas. The Kiowa-Apaches **allied** with the Kiowa tribe on the Plains.

CATTLE RAIDS

No longer able to hunt buffalo on Comanche land, the other Plains Apaches looked for new sources of food. Soon their whole economy changed to one based on raiding Spanish ranches for horses and cattle to use as food. By the time Mexico gained its independence from Spain, in 1821, Apache raiding was a serious problem in northern Mexico (which included the present-day U.S. states of Arizona and New Mexico).

> The supplying of drink [whiskey] to the Indians will be a means of gaining their goodwill, discovering their secrets, calming them so they will think less of [engaging in] hostilities, and . . . will oblige them to recognize their dependence upon us more directly.
>
> *Bernardo de Galvez, 1786, Spanish Viceroy of Mexico*

> I do not think you will keep the peace. . . . [Y]ou tell me we can stay in our mountains and our valleys. . . . We want nothing but to live in peace. But I do not believe you will allow us to remain on the lands we love.
>
> I warn you, if you try to move us again, war will start once more; it will be a war without end, a war in which every Apache will fight until he is dead.
>
> *Apache chief Cochise to U.S. General O. O. Howard, who had promised the Apaches in 1872 that they could stay in peace on their own land. That promise died with Cochise.*

THE AMERICANS ARRIVE

In 1848, the United States won a war with Mexico, claiming much of the Apache homeland, including Arizona and New Mexico, which previously belonged to its southern neighbor. Americans began pouring into the region, causing problems for the Apaches — the Americans had little respect for Apache rights to the land.

THE END OF AN ERA

Over the next forty years, the Apache groups were rounded up and forced onto reservations. Many Apaches fought against U.S. government troops in

Apaches were masters at blending in with their environment. They could disappear in the desert and be nearly impossible to find and then suddenly appear to spring an **ambush**.

Cochise (1812 – 1874)

Cochise became the most famous Apache war chief during the 1860s. By age twenty-three, he was a war leader of the Chiricahua Apaches. He quickly gained fame for his daring raids on Mexican ranches and towns. When Americans entered the Southwest, Cochise tried to stay at peace with them. In 1861, however, Lieutenant George Bascom accused Cochise of raiding in the United States and arrested him, even though Cochise had come to talk under a white flag of **truce**. Cochise escaped and for ten years led Apache warriors against U.S. troops in a bloody war. He signed a peace treaty in 1872 and lived peacefully until his death in 1874.

Cochise was widely respected as both a war leader and a voice for peace. When he died, he was trying to find a way for his people to live peacefully with the Americans.

defense of their homelands. By the 1880s, however, only some Western Apaches remained outside the reservation system. Even those Apaches confined to the reservations often left to wage war in protest over the overcrowding, sickness, and poor food on the reservations.

Finally, in 1886, Geronimo and his small band of followers became the last Apaches to surrender. They were sent to Florida as prisoners of war. Open **hostilities** between Apaches and Americans came to an end and the reservation era began.

RESERVATION LIFE

When the Indian wars were over, the U.S. government used the reservation system to try to force Indians to adopt white values. It was a grim time for the Apache people and their culture.

Mescalero Apaches in 1919 on the Mescalero reservation in New Mexico. It would be many years before the Mescaleros began to recover from the harsh conditions of the early reservation years.

> Take stones and ashes and thorns and, with some scorpions and rattlesnakes thrown in, dump the outfit on stones, heat the stones red-hot, set the United States Army after the Apaches, and you have San Carlos.
>
> *Daklugie, nephew of Geronimo, describing San Carlos Apache Reservation*

The change to reservation life was very difficult. Poverty, lack of jobs, despair, and poor food caused serious health problems. Apache populations declined at alarming rates. The population of the Jicarilla Apaches, for example, dropped from 995 in 1905 to only 588 in 1920. By 1920, nearly 90 percent of the Jicarilla children suffered from tuberculosis, a serious lung disease.

It was one of the worst periods in American history for Native Americans, a time when Indians did not have many rights, not even freedom of religion. The government was determined to end Indian culture and make Indians just like everyone else, a process called **acculturation**.

APACHES TAKING CONTROL

These attitudes began to change in the 1930s when Congress passed the Indian Reorganization Act, which allowed the Apaches

Apache children were taken from their families and sent away to harsh boarding schools where they were forbidden to speak their language and dress in Apache clothing.

and other Indian tribes to form tribal governments again. It was not until 1978, however, that the U.S. government passed the American Indian Religious Freedom Act.

Other laws since then have made it easier for tribal governments to operate businesses. Apache tribes have taken advantage of these changes and today are working to try to improve the lives of their people.

Chapter 3

TRADITIONAL WAY OF LIFE

TRADITIONAL ECONOMY

As European-Americans moved onto Native American lands, Indian tribes were forced to adapt dramatically. One of the most remarkable adaptations was how the Apaches shifted their economy from one based on hunting buffalo to one based on raiding Spanish ranches. Apaches became so successful at it that the Spanish in northern Mexico complained that they were practically working for the Apaches.

LIGHTNING-QUICK RAIDS

The Spanish worked all year raising herds of horses, cattle, sheep, and mules. Then, suddenly, the Apaches would sweep down from the north and steal them.

Apache raids sometimes occurred hundreds of miles into Mexico. The raiders often went on foot to their target, traveling through the

An Apache warrior traveled light. Whether on foot or on horseback, Apaches skillfully made their way over the rugged, mountainous terrain of the Southwest.

Apaches became the most skillful raiders in the history of North America. No one knew when or where they would strike, and trying to catch them was nearly impossible.

most rugged, isolated **terrain**, avoiding contact with anyone and maintaining the element of surprise.

Striking quickly, the Apaches moved the stolen livestock northward at a pace that amazed their pursuers. If the pursuers got too close, some of the Apaches laid ambushes for them, while others continued herding the livestock northward. Once they had reached their home territory, they divided up the livestock and then scattered into the vastness of the landscape, in small groups again, making it virtually impossible for the Spanish, and later for the Mexicans, to pursue them farther. Apache raiding virtually halted the advance of Spanish settlement northward from Mexico.

An Apache bride, dressed for her wedding day. Apache women are a source of strength for their people, respected for their knowledge and hard work.

Apache raiding was so successful that they had very little reason to attempt to become farmers or ranchers. Even by the late 1800s, the United States had trouble convincing the Apaches to farm or ranch.

TRADITIONAL LIFE

Apache traditional culture is matrilineal, meaning that a family tree is traced through the mother's family. When an Apache man married, he went to live with his wife's family and her relatives. Children of the marriage automatically belonged to the wife's **clan**.

An Apache mother-in-law was forbidden to talk to the husband of her daughter. This helped to avoid conflict in the household between a husband and his mother-in-law.

Apaches lived and traveled most of the year in small units of related families, with little traditional formal government. The group was led by someone who was chosen by the others. A leader could lose that position by making foolish decisions or putting the group in danger.

TRADITIONAL CRAFTS

Apache women were skilled at making a kind of basket called a twined **burden** basket. To make them, they coiled reeds and grasses into stout containers to carry nuts and roots. They also made sandals from mescal fibers.

Many of the Apache crafts fell into disuse during the reservation era when the United States established trading houses for the Apaches. They became dependent upon pots and pans and other manufactured goods, instead of their own handiwork. However, baskets and sandals are still made today and are sold in the tribal gift shops.

Apache basket making is a fine art. The baskets are not only beautiful but practical as well. Apache sandals made from mescal fibers were perfectly suited to the desert.

Apache Housing

Eastern Apaches lived in **tepees** made of buffalo hides, even after they lost the buffalo plains to the Comanches and had to trade with other Indians to get the hides. Western Apaches, however, invented a structure, called a wickiup, that was perfect for their land. Branches were woven together into a round frame and then covered with desert bushes and leaves. Providing shade in the desert heat, the wickiup could be built quickly, with materials readily at hand, and then quickly abandoned, making the Apaches highly **mobile**. It was also nearly invisible because it blended in with the other bushes so well, making an Apache camp hard to find.

APACHE CHILDHOOD

Apache children began training in how to survive in their harsh land as soon as they were old enough to walk. Each morning, an Apache elder in the camp would wake the children at sunrise and send them running to the top of a hill and back. As they grew older, they were required to carry a mouthful of water the whole way without losing any.

Apache girls played with dolls made of corn husks. The dolls are dressed in leather clothing.

On summer mornings, the children would also be made to swim in the ice-cold mountain streams. On winter mornings, they would be made to roll naked in the snow.

By the time Apache children were teenagers, they had learned to withstand cold, heat, hunger, and thirst that few other humans could endure. They were so **agile** that they could run through the rough terrain of their landscape farther and faster than soldiers mounted on horseback.

Apache babies on cradleboards. The cradleboards left the mother free to perform her work while keeping the babies safe.

Apache chief Antonio Maria with his family in 1897. The family is dressed in their finest clothing for the photograph.

A NATION OF ATHLETES

This training produced some the most exceptional **guerrilla warfare** fighters in history. Even as old men, Apache warriors such as Geronimo were superior athletes to the young soldiers who tried to catch them.

For Apache children — and for many adults — footraces were by far the most important of the Apache sports. Men competed against men, women against women, and children against children. Today, this tradition continues as an important part of annual Apache gatherings, most notably among the Jicarilla Apaches in northern New Mexico and the Mescalero Apaches in southeastern New Mexico.

APACHE BELIEFS

Traditional Apache life includes a belief in a Creator, the Life Giver, who might respond to prayers and aid in dealing with problems. Through ceremonies and prayers, some Apache men and women sought a variety of powers. Some of those powers included the ability to know what was happening at a distance, the power to surprise and defeat an enemy, the power to make the wind blow to create a dust storm to hide from an enemy, and the power to make the horses more gentle. These Apaches became **spiritual** leaders, whom others consulted.

Ceremonial grounds of the White Mountain Apaches on the Fort Apache Reservation in Arizona. The traditional dances performed on the ceremonial grounds help preserve a sense of community in Apache culture.

DEATH, BE NOT NAMED

Apaches never talked about death and never referred to dead people by name. If death was mentioned during the preparations for a war party, the war party would be canceled. Upon the death of a parent, the children's names would be changed so they would not have to recall how the parent had used their name.

> We had no churches, no religious organizations, no **sabbath** day, no holidays, and yet we worshipped. Sometimes the whole tribe would assemble to sing and pray; sometimes in a smaller number, perhaps only two or three. . . . Sometimes we prayed in silence; sometimes each one prayed aloud; sometimes an aged person prayed for all of us.
>
> *Geronimo in his book,* Geronimo's Story of His Life

Apache dancers perform the Mountain Spirit Dance in Gallup, New Mexico.

When an Apache died, the body was buried as quickly as possible and the camp was moved. It was believed that illness could be spread by viewing the body or by touching that person's possessions. Everything that person owned was hastily buried with the body.

Apaches also avoided the topic of owls, which they believed were the ghosts of dead people. An owl's hooting caused serious concern in an Apache camp. There were no jokes in the culture regarding owls and no stories about them. Like death, owls were a topic to be avoided.

Today, important Apache ceremonies continue to be performed on the reservations, including the Apache Fire Dance and the Mountain Spirit Dance, which celebrate the continuation of Apache culture.

Fox Steals Fire

This story is told by the Apaches to explain how they came to use fire for cooking and keeping warm. The main character in this story is Fox, a cunning figure found in many Apache stories.

Long ago in a time before people had fire, some geese were teaching Fox how to fly. They made him wings but they warned him to keep his eyes shut or he would fall out of the sky.

One day, Fox and the geese flew around until it was dark. They passed over a village of fireflies far below them on the ground. Even with his eyes shut, Fox was aware of the glare of their fire and he opened his eyes. At that moment, his wings broke into pieces, and Fox fell to the ground. He landed in the center of the fireflies' walled village, close to where the fire burned.

The fireflies were friendly and told Fox he could escape over the wall if he wanted to. All he had to do was ask a cedar tree to bend down, and if he clung on tightly, it would catapult him over the wall.

Fox was desperate to get hold of fire, so he thought up a cunning plan. He suggested that the fireflies should hold a dance and he would play music for them. Fox went away and made himself a drum. He also tied a strip of cedar bark to his tail. That night, as the fireflies danced, Fox moved slowly closer to the fire.

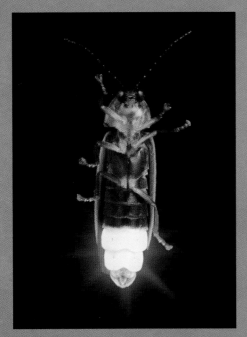

We know today that the light produced by fireflies is certainly not fire. In fact, it is not even hot. When several chemical substances in the fireflies' bodies come into contact with each other, they produce light.

Suddenly, he swept his tail into the fire and lit the bark. Then he ran to the cedar tree, shouting for it to bend down. As it lowered its branches, Fox caught hold of one of them, and he was carried over the wall.

Fox ran and ran, chased by the angry fireflies. When he was tired he gave the burning bark to Hawk, who flew away with it. Eventually, Hawk too was tired, so he gave the bark to Crane, who flew southward for hundreds of miles. As Crane flew, he dropped sparks all over the earth for people to use, until he came to the lands of the Apaches.

Fox, however, never benefited from his cleverness. The fireflies punished him by making him unable to use fire for himself.

The crane of this story is the species called the sandhill crane. It breeds in the northern United States and Canada and migrates in winter to the southwestern United States and Mexico. The Apaches saw that the cranes arrived from the north every year, and so this migration became part of their story.

APACHE LIFE TODAY

APACHE AUTHORS

Apaches have made important contributions to Native American **scholarship**, literature, and the arts. Jicarilla Apache scholar Veronica E. Velarde Tiller became the first Apache to write a scholarly history of her people, titled *The Jicarilla Apache Tribe*, which concentrates on the problems her people have faced in the twentieth century.

White Mountain Apache poet Roman C. Adrian's poetry has appeared in many publications, including *The Remembered Earth*. The first major collection of native literature, this book was published in the late 1960s and is widely used in college courses in Native American literature. The late Chiricahua

A painted hide by Apache artist Joseph Skywolf. Hide paintings were sometimes used to record historic events by the tribe.

Apache poet Blossom Haozous published traditional Apache stories in both the Apache language and English, including Apache origin stories. In contrast, Jicarilla Apache creative writers Stacey Velarde and Carson Vicenti write stories about modern life, revealing the problems and joys of being an Indian in today's world.

Mescalero Apache Lorenzo Baca is among the most talented creative artists, working in video, sculpture, art, storytelling, and acting. His "round poems" are circle poems, cleverly constructed and fun to read. Baca's poetry has been published in several collections of poetry, and he has also made audio recordings.

Geronimo

Geronimo was not only the most famous Apache war leader and **medicine man**, but he is also the most famous Apache author. To a translator and a secretary, he dictated *Geronimo's Story of His Life*, one of the most widely read books written by any Indian. He had become so famous by that time that his appearance at the St. Louis World's Fair in 1905, while he was still a prisoner of war, created a sensation. At the World's Fair, he sold photos of himself for ten cents each. He died in prison of pneumonia at Fort Sill, Oklahoma, in 1909.

Apache leader Geronimo (right) with three of his warriors, in Arizona in the 1880s. Geronimo and his Chiricahua band were not allowed to remain in Arizona.

A World-Famous Artist

By far the most famous Apache artist, Chiricahua Apache sculptor Allan Houser (1914–1994) received worldwide recognition for his work in marble, bronze, wood, and stone. Houser became famous for his large sculptures, many now in the permanent collections of museums and universities throughout the world. His work won many awards, including the Prix de West Award of the National Cowboy Hall of Fame for his sculpture *Smoke Signals*. One of his best-known works is *As Long as the Waters Flow*, a bronze statue of an Indian woman, which stands outside the state capitol (government building) in Oklahoma City.

In the 1980s, Houser and his son Philip created a sculpture garden in Santa Fe, New Mexico. Visitors can walk around ten acres of sculpture trails and admire more than eighty Houser sculptures.

In 2009, a picture of Houser's sculpture *Sacred Rain Arrow* was chosen to decorate new Oklahoma state motor vehicle license plates.

Apache sculptor Allan Houser with one of his large sculptures, in bronze.

32

Salt River Canyon on the San Carlos Apache Reservation in Arizona. Most of San Carlos is harsh, arid land similar to that shown here.

THE WESTERN APACHES

Most Apaches in Arizona live on reservations. The two biggest reservations, the San Carlos Apache Reservation and the Fort Apache Reservation, are close together in eastern Arizona. Home to about seven thousand Western Apaches today, the San Carlos Apache Reservation is one of the poorest places in the United States. One fourth of the workforce have no jobs, and 60 percent of the people live in poverty.

The tribe lost most of what little farmland was available when part of the reservation was flooded following the building of the Coolidge Dam in 1930. Most of the land today is desert, mountain meadows, or pine forests.

In recent years, tribal members have made some income by mining **semiprecious** stones such as peridot and by a limited amount of farming. Tourists also come to the reservation to hunt, fish, play golf, or gamble. The building of the Coolidge Dam created San Carlos Lake on the reservation, and today the San Carlos Apaches sell permits to fishers, hikers, and campers.

This statue overlooks the San Carlos Apache golf course in Arizona. The San Carlos Apaches are attempting to increase their income from tourists.

The San Carlos Apache Cultural Center opened in Peridot in 1995. Its exhibits feature Apache religion and ceremonies. The center also promotes and sells the work of Apache craftspeople.

TRIBES OF THE FORT APACHE RESERVATION

The Fort Apache Reservation in eastern Arizona is home to the Coyotero Apaches and also includes the Cibeque and White Mountain Apaches, a total population of about nine thousand. Originally, the reservation contained the largest forest of ponderosa pine trees in the world, but American logging companies were allowed to cut the trees, with very little benefit to the Apaches. Today, the Fort Apache Timber Company in Whiteriver processes low-grade timber from its two sawmills. In 2003, massive wildfires on the reservation destroyed large areas of woodland, which the Apaches were managing for timber.

In 1954, the tribe founded the Fort Apache Recreational Enterprise, leading to much economic activity, including building a ski area and summer resort. The mountains, lakes, and fishing streams lure tourists and their money, boosting tribal income and employment. Permits are sold for white-water rafting, kayaking, and canoeing on Salt River. Farming and cattle raising are also important. The most successful tribal business, however, has been its casino, which lures gamblers by the thousands. The casino opened in 1993 and was so successful it was doubled in size in 1995.

The Fort Apache White Mountain Cultural Center is another tourist attraction. It showcases Apache historic objects as well as exhibiting modern Apache arts and crafts. Outside the center are the old Fort Apache buildings, begun in 1870, and a recreation of an Apache village.

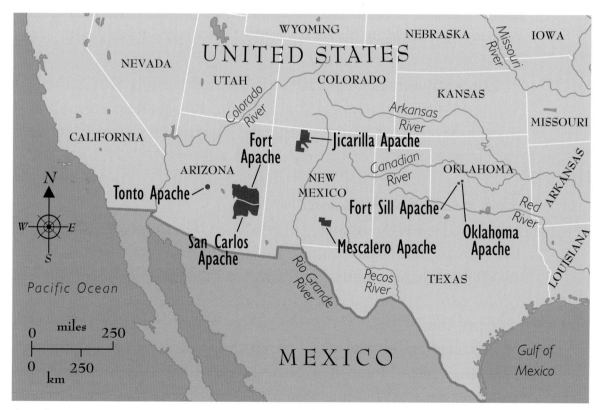

Apache reservations in Arizona, New Mexico, and Oklahoma.

A young Apache girl on horseback at the Fort Apache Reservation.

For many Western Apaches, the highlight of the year is the White Mountain Apache Tribal Fair and Rodeo, held annually in early September, where people get together to take part in a variety of competitions, parades, and a carnival.

THE EASTERN APACHES

In 1936, the Kiowa-Apaches in western Oklahoma joined with the Kiowas to form a business council for the tribes. Today, the two tribes operate many programs for their people, including health care and educational programs for the children.

Until the 1930s, the Mescalero Apaches of southeastern New Mexico had leased their land to white ranchers for cattle grazing. They then began their own cattle-raising operation, increasing tribal revenue from $18,000 to $101,000 during their first three years. Timber sales also provide tribal income.

In 1963, the Mescaleros bought a nearby ski area. Since then, they have turned it into a year-round tourist attraction, with a large hotel, tennis courts, restaurants, and a golf course.

In the mountains of northern New Mexico, the Jicarilla Apaches benefited from the discovery of oil on their reservation in the 1950s. By the 1990s, tribal revenue from the oil was $11 million a year. Today, there are more than two thousand oil and gas wells on Jicarilla land.

In the 1980s, Jicarilla parents began getting elected to their school board and demanding better education for their children. In 1988, the Jicarilla school district was chosen New Mexico School District of the Year.

An Eastern Apache traditional drummer and singer. The drum is at the very heart of traditional Apache dances.

CURRENT ISSUES

Apaches on all the reservations have made great strides in recent decades to overcome the difficulties that threatened their existence as a people, but some threats remain.

THREATS TO APACHE HOMELANDS

In Arizona, the San Carlos Apaches are fighting to prevent a Southeast Arizona Land Exchange **Bill** from becoming law. This bill would take away some of their most **sacred** land and give it to a copper mining company.

In Texas, the Lipan Apache Women Defense group was set up in 2007 to investigate human rights abuses by the U.S. government against native people in the Lower Rio Grande River area of Texas. The U.S. government is taking land from people along the border with Mexico to build a fence between the two countries.

Mount Graham

Mount Graham, in eastern Arizona, is a sacred site for the San Carlos Apaches. In 1988, Congress allowed the University of Arizona, the German Max Planck Institute, the Italian Arcetri Observatory, and the Vatican to build telescopes on Mount Graham. The San Carlos Apache Tribal Council tried unsuccessfully in both the U.S. Congress and the courts to stop the construction. Despite studies that show Mount Graham to be a poor place for using telescopes, three large telescopes are now in use there.

The Sunrise Ceremony

A young Apache woman's **puberty** ceremony, called Na'ii'ees, or the "Sunrise Ceremony," is a **ritual** portrayal of the Apache origin story. The ceremony requires a day of preparation, including a sweat bath, a gift of food to relatives, presentation of the girl by a medicine man, and a ceremonial dance. She also runs four laps to represent the four stages of her life. For four days after the ceremony, the girl is considered holy. She is believed to take on the powers of Changing Woman, from the Apache origin story, with power to cure the sick and bring rain.

An Apache girl running laps around ceremonial grounds.

LOOKING TO THE FUTURE

The Apache population is now increasing and is in the tens of thousands. The survival of their people, and their culture, is a **testament** to their strength. They still face many problems, but they are facing those challenges and looking to the future with hope for a better life for their people.

TIMELINE

800–900	Period when Apaches may have migrated into the Southwest from the north.
1275–1300	Severe, prolonged drought in the Southwest causes ancient civilizations to abandon most of the land. Apaches may have migrated into the region after this time.
1540s–1590	Spanish expeditions of Francisco de Coronado and others explore the Southwest, leaving accounts of the Apaches.
1598	Spanish settle New Mexico permanently and disrupt trade relations between Apaches and Pueblo Indians.
early 1700s	The Comanche migration to the Southern Plains from Wyoming pushes most Plains Apaches off the Plains, except for the Kiowa-Apaches and the Lipan Apaches.
about 1724	Apaches lose great battle with Comanches for control of the southern Plains.
late 1700s and early 1800s	Plains Apaches survive by raiding Spanish ranches for horses and cattle.
1848	U.S. war with Mexico ends; Southwest becomes U.S. territory.
1850s–86	The Apaches fight wars with the United States as white settlers pour into their homelands.
1870s–80s	Most Apaches are confined to reservations; only some Western Apaches remain outside the reservations.
1886	Geronimo surrenders and is sent to Florida as prisoner of war, along with 468 other Apaches.
1887	Kiowa-Apache lands in Indian Territory are opened to American settlers.
1909	Geronimo dies in prison.

1920	Conditions on reservations are so bad that almost 90 percent of Jicarilla children have tuberculosis.
1930	Most of the farmland on the San Carlos Apache reservation is flooded following the building of the Coolidge Dam.
1934	Apache tribal governments are formed under the Indian Reorganization Act.
1936	Kiowa-Apaches in western Oklahoma join with the Kiowas to form a business council.
1950s	Oil is discovered on the Jicarilla Reservation in New Mexico.
1954	Fort Apache Recreation Enterprise is started to increase economic activity.
1963	Mescalero Apache tribe buys a ski area to make into a resort.
1988	Jicarilla school district is chosen New Mexico School District of the Year. Congress allows the building of telescopes on the sacred site of Mount Graham, Arizona, against the wishes of the Apaches.
1993	Fort Apache casino opens.
1994	San Carlos Apache tribe opens casino in Arizona.
1995	San Carlos Apache Cultural Center opens in Peridot.
2001	A judge in Arizona allows telescope construction to continue on Mount Graham.
2003	Sixty percent of commercial forests in the Fort Apache Reservation are destroyed by a massive wildfire.
2007	Lipan Apache Women Defense group is set up to protect Native peoples and their land in the border area between the United States and Mexico, where a fence is being built.
2011	San Carlos Apaches oppose the Southeast Arizona Land Exchange Bill, which would give some of their most sacred land to Resolution Copper mining company.

GLOSSARY

acculturation: the process of forcing one group to adopt the culture—the language, lifestyle, and values—of another.

adaptable: able to change to suit new conditions or surroundings.

agile: able to move and react quickly and easily.

allied: worked or fought together.

ambush: a surprise attack by people who are waiting in hiding.

ancestors: people from whom an individual or group is descended.

bill: a proposed law.

boarding schools: places where students must live at the school.

burden: a load; something that is carried.

civilization: the society, culture, and way of life of a people.

clan: a group of related families.

culture: the arts, beliefs, and customs that make up a people's way of life.

degradation: a state of being treated with disrespect or contempt.

dialect: a type of language that is spoken in a particular area or by a particular group of people.

discrimination: unjust treatment, usually because of a person's race or sex.

drought: a long period of little rain.

economy: the way a country or people produces, divides up, and uses its goods and money.

environment: objects and conditions all around that affect living things and communities.

floodplain: the area of land beside a river or stream that is covered with water during a flood.

guerrilla warfare: a kind of war in which small groups of people make lightning-quick, surprise attacks.

hostilities: acts of war.

ice age: a period of time when the earth is very cold and lots of water in the oceans turns to ice.

irrigation: any system for watering the land to grow plants.

medicine man: a spiritual or religious leader.

migration: movement from one place to another.

mobile: able to move easily.

persecution: treating someone or a certain group of people badly over a period of time.

poverty: the state of being very poor.

prejudice: dislike or injustice that is not based on reason or experience.

puberty: the time of physical changes in the body when a girl becomes a woman or a boy becomes a man, usually during the early teenage years.

reservation: land set aside by the U.S. government for specific Native American tribes to live on.

ritual: a system of special ceremonies.

sabbath: a day each week when people do not work in the Jewish and Christian religions.

sacred: having to do with religion or spirituality.

scholarship: advanced study and learning.

semiprecious: describes gems that are less valuable than diamonds, rubies, and emeralds.

spiritual: affecting the human spirit or religion rather than physical things.

tepee: a cone-shaped tent supported by long, slender pine poles and draped with buffalo hides.

terrain: an area with distinctive physical features.

testament: proof.

treaty: an agreement among two or more nations.

truce: an agreement between enemies to stop fighting.

MORE RESOURCES

WEBSITES:

http://impurplehawk.com/index.html
> An award-winning website including Apache music, photos, and information on many aspects of Apache life.

http://www.allanhouser.com/
> A site devoted to the life and work of the sculptor Allan Houser.

http://www.bigorrin.org/apache_kids.htm
> Online Apache Indian Fact Sheet For Kids in question-and-answer form with useful links.

http://www.brooklynmuseum.org/opencollection/artists/2740/Apache
> Photos of historic Apache clothing and artifacts from the Brooklyn Museum.

http://www.desertusa.com/ind1/du_peo_apache.html
> A detailed history of the Western Apaches.

http://www.firstpeople.us/FP-Html-Legends/Geronimo_His_Own _Story_1.html
> Geronimo's own account of Apache culture and traditional life.

http://www.fortsillapache-nsn.gov/index.php?option=com_ content&view=article&id=5&Itemid=6
> The website of the Fort Sill Apaches of Oklahoma includes a detailed history of the tribe and interesting information about famous people, traditional clothing, food, shelters, and jewelry.

http://nativeamericans.mrdonn.org/southwest/apache.html
> A site for younger children about the traditional daily life of the Western Apaches.

http://www.native-languages.org/apache.htm
> A guide to the Apache language, including vocabulary.

http://www.native-languages.org/apache-legends.htm
> A brief description of Apache mythological figures plus many links to Apache legends and traditional stories and to books on Apache mythology.

http://www.texasindians.com/ap2.htm
A site mainly about the Apaches in Texas and their interaction with Spanish missions.

DVD:
American Experience: Geronimo and the Apache Resistance. PBS, 2007.

BOOKS:
Behnke, Alison. *The Apaches (Native American Histories).* Lerner Publications, 2006.

Feinstein, Stephen. *Read About Geronimo (I Like Biographies!).* Enslow Elementary, 2006.

Friedmann, Mark, and Peter Benoit. *The Apache (True Books).* Children's Press, 2011.

Gibson, Karen Bush. *Native American History for Kids: With 21 Activities.* Chicago Review Press, 2010.

Goble, Paul. *Tipi: Home of the Nomadic Buffalo Hunters.* World Wisdom, 2007.

Haugen, Brenda. *Geronimo: Apache Warrior (Signature Lives: American Frontier Era).* Compass Point Books, 2006.

King, David C. *First People.* DK Children, 2008.

Kissock, Heather, and Jordan McGill. *Apache (American Indian Art and Culture).* Weigl Publishers, 2010.

Miller, Raymond H. *The Apache (North American Indians).* Kidhaven, 2005.

Moody, Ralph. *Geronimo: Wolf of the Warpath.* Sterling, 2006.

Murdoch, David S. *North American Indian (DK Eyewitness Books).* DK Children, 2005.

Phillips, Larissa. *Cochise: Apache Chief (Primary Sources of Famous People in American History).* Rosen Publishing Group, 2003.

Sonneborn, Liz. *The Apache (Watts Library).* Children's Press, 2005.

Sullivan, George. *Geronimo: Apache Renegade (Sterling Biographies).* Sterling, 2010.

Worth, Richard. *The Apache: A Proud People (American Indians).* Enslow Elementary, 2005.

THINGS TO THINK ABOUT AND DO

BUFFALO = HORSES + CATTLE?

The ranches in the Apaches' homeland were established without their permission. Why might Apaches think of horses and cattle on the white men's ranches as a substitute for buffalo on the plains?

Write a paragraph explaining what you think.

TEPEES AND WICKIUPS

Draw a picture of what an Apache camp might have looked like.

How would an Eastern Apache camp, with its tepees, look different from a Western Apache camp, with its wickiups?

SCHOOLED AWAY FROM HOME

What kind of problems do you think an Apache child might have at a faraway, military-style boarding school run by the U.S. government, and how would life be different at an ordinary school near home?

INDEX